AUSET GYPSY TAROT

CREATED BY
JAMES JACOB PIERRI

ILLUSTRATED BY
REBECCA STOTSENBURGH AND
HEATHER SCOTT

REDFeather™
MIND | BODY | SPIRIT

4880 Lower Valley Road, Atglen, PA 19310

Other Schiffer Books on Related Subjects:
Ostara Tarot, Molly Applejohn, Eden Cooke, Krista Gibbard, and Julia Iredale, ISBN 978-0-7643-5282-9
Spirit within Tarot, Steven Bright, ISBN 978-0-7643-5388-8

Copyright © 2021 by James Jacob Pierri

Library of Congress Control Number: 2020914742

All rights reserved. No part of this work may be reproduced or used in any form or by any means—graphic, electronic, or mechanical, including photocopying or information storage and retrieval systems—without written permission from the publisher.

The scanning, uploading, and distribution of this book or any part thereof via the Internet or any other means without the permission of the publisher is illegal and punishable by law. Please purchase only authorized editions and do not participate in or encourage the electronic piracy of copyrighted materials.

"Red Feather Mind Body Spirit" logo is a trademark of Schiffer Publishing, Ltd.
"Red Feather Mind Body Spirit Feather" logo is a registered trademark of Schiffer Publishing, Ltd.

Cover and interior design by Jack Chappell
Type set in Charcuterie Block/Litania/Minion Pro

ISBN: 978-0-7643-6152-4
Printed in China

Published by Red Feather Mind, Body, Spirit
An imprint of Schiffer Publishing, Ltd.
4880 Lower Valley Road
Atglen, PA 19310
Phone: (610) 593-1777; Fax: (610) 593-2002
E-mail: Info@schifferbooks.com
Web: www.redfeathermbs.com

For our complete selection of fine books on this and related subjects, please visit our website at www.schifferbooks.com. You may also write for a free catalog.

Schiffer Publishing's titles are available at special discounts for bulk purchases for sales promotions or premiums. Special editions, including personalized covers, corporate imprints, and excerpts, can be created in large quantities for special needs. For more information, contact the publisher.

We are always looking for people to write books on new and related subjects. If you have an idea for a book, please contact us at proposals@schifferbooks.com.

THIS TAROT DECK AND ALL ITS WORK AND MYSTERIES ARE DEDICATED TO MY MUSE, THE GODDESS ISIS, WITH LOVE, THANKS, AND DEVOTION.

IN ADDITION, THIS DECK IS ALSO DEDICATED TO TAROT ENTHUSIASTS EVERYWHERE: THOSE JUST BEGINNING THEIR EXPERIENCE AND THOSE SEASONED PROFESSIONALS STILL CONTINUING THE JOURNEY!

THANK YOU FROM THE BOTTOM OF MY HEART TO MY FAMILY, FRIENDS, MENTORS, AND LOVED ONES FOR THEIR CONTINUAL CONTRIBUTIONS AND SUPPORT.

Table of Contents

Foreword	6
The Story of the Auset Gypsy Tarot	8
The Major Arcana	10
Number 0: The Fool	12
Number 1: The Magician	14
Number 2: The High Priestess	16
Number 3: The Empress	18
Number 4: The Emperor	20
Number 5: The Hierophant	22
Number 6: The Lovers	24
Number 7: The Chariot	26
Number 8: Justice	28
Number 9: The Hermit	30
Number 10: Wheel of Fortune	32
Number 11: Strength	34
Number 12: The Hanged Man	36
Number 13: Death (Dance Macabre)	38
Number 14: Temperance	40
Number 15: The Devil	42
Number 16: The Tower	44
Number 17: The Star	46
Number 18: The Moon	48
Number 19: The Sun	50
Number 20: Judgement (Fame & Fortune)	52
Number 21: The World	54

The Minor Arcana		56
Ace of Cups	Ace of Wands	57
Ace of Coins	Ace of Swords	58
2 of Cups	2 of Wands	59
2 of Coins	2 of Swords	60
3 of Cups	3 of Wands	61
3 of Coins	3 of Swords	62
4 of Cups	4 of Wands	63
4 of Coins	4 of Swords	64
5 of Cups	5 of Wands	65
5 of Coins	5 of Swords	66
6 of Cups	6 of Wands	67
6 of Coins	6 of Swords	68
7 of Cups	7 of Wands	69
7 of Coins	7 of Swords	70
8 of Cups	8 of Wands	71
8 of Coins	8 of Swords	72
9 of Cups	9 of Wands	73
9 of Coins	9 of Swords	74
10 of Cups	10 of Wands	75
10 of Coins	10 of Swords	76
King of Cups	Queen of Cups	77
Cavalier of Cups	Prince/ess of Cups	78
King of Wands	Queen of Wands	79
Cavalier of Wands	Prince/ess of Wands	80
King of Coins	Queen of Coins	81
Cavalier of Coins	Prince/ess of Coins	82
King of Swords	Queen of Swords	83
Cavalier of Swords	Prince/ess of Swords	84

Auset Gypsy Tarot Spreads	85
Auset Gypsy Tarot Advice, Mantras, and Practices to Live by and Meditate On	92
Notes	94
About the Author	96

FOREWORD

The cards speak!

Hear them, listen to them! Respect them. From the moment that first card is drawn and thrown, the language of the Tarot speaks directly to the spirit and soul.

Sometimes in images; other times it could be words. It's all a unique and personal experience. There's no right or wrong way to read. The Tarot will instruct you if you let them.

The Auset Gypsy Tarot Deck is charged with many layers. Symbols, images, astrology, traditional definitions, and some new points of view. Many choices! Choices are what the Tarot is all about.

The Auset Gypsy Tarot Deck has been a lifetime in the making! I began reading Tarot on the streets of major cities such as New York and Miami, to name a couple. Over time I was invited to read and teach Tarot in popular major destination spots—metaphysical centers, shops, museums, colleges, and libraries—both nationally and internationally, including such world-renowned cities as Orlando, Florida; San Francisco, California; Rio De Janeiro, Brazil; and London, England. Top event and entertainment agencies hired me to read for celebrities, professional athletes, politicians, and famous musicians at private events. I had become a famous fortune teller! In the interim I also became a published astrologer with Auset Gypsy–branded horoscope columns in international fashion magazines. Radio, podcasts, and TV were also part of my repertoire. However, underneath all of that public recognition and excitement, the most important focus was always the integrity of the Tarot readings and perpetual pursuit of metaphysical and spiritual study, practice, and meditation. At a very young age I was given the opportunity to become a full-time professional Tarot reader at one of the world's most recognized entertainment destinations.

I showed up to the interview with a marked-up (meaning I added my own astrological symbols and sigils to the cards in pen), old-fashioned Cagliostro Tarot Deck that impressed my soon-to-be new boss. That moment opened the door to the World for this young Fool.

This Auset Gypsy Tarot Deck is reminiscent of my old deck that started my journey and career and contains the story of my experience and adventure. The choice of rich, bold colors and a modern, artistic style is an important element for this deck. That's why choosing artists Rebecca Stotsenburgh and Heather Scott as the illustrators to bring my original concepts and sketches to life was the perfect choice. Both offer a fresh style that's romantic yet current. I want readers of the day to enjoy something new and modern, and for readers in the future to have something reminiscent of this time and era. Such decisions are crucial when contributing to the generations-long tapestry of Tarot history. Every character tells their own story, and every detail supports it!

I hope it brings you, the reader, as much inspiration, adventure, romance, mystery, and joy that the Tarot has brought me.

One final reminder! Remember it's a spiritual and ethical responsibility once you open your first deck of Tarot cards and announce to the world that you read the cards. Everyone from the most devout believer to the most pessimistic naysayer will be influenced by what is seen in the cards, so become friends with your deck, practice diligently, learn its language, and, most importantly, always be honest with yourself and the questioner. Good luck and Let the Adventure Begin . . .

Sincerely,
James Jacob Pierri

For more info go to:
AusetGypsy.com

THE STORY OF THE AUSET GYPSY TAROT

Auset: [syll. AU-set, AUS-et] An
ancient Egyptian pronunciation of
the name of the Goddess Isis

Gypsy: [gyp·sy / ˈjipsē/] A nomadic
or free-spirited person

The Fool card through the World card is the story of the Tarot as it has been relayed for generations, and it's the most popular explanation of the Major Arcana. But this is the Auset Gypsy Tarot Deck and it's a new story, a different telling, true to tradition but with its own unique adventure!

And like all classic stories, ours begins like this . . .

Once upon a time in a mythical place on an enchanted island full of magic, mystery, fascinating locales, and colorful inhabitants, a stranger appeared. This wanderer, coming out of nowhere, came with a driving ambition to traverse this island's magical geography, learn its secrets, unravel the mysteries, and master his fate! He knew this was where he belonged.

Our hero explored every special place, met face to face with gods, was tricked by spirits, and conquered many trials and tribulations. He accumulated many metaphysical and arcane skills offered from each experience. Eventually feeling satisfied, he decided to settle down.

Here on this island there was an eternal and stationary carnival. It was where most of the inhabitants lived, and there was an unending supply of visitors frequenting this robust carnival of life, filled to the brim with stringed lights glowing about, rich colorful tents, and incredible performers everywhere! Every corner held hints of romance and even danger.

It was a place found in dreams, and sometimes things weren't always what they seemed.

The wanderer found himself happily nestled between all of this day-and-night revelry. He offered his skills of divination or fortune telling, of which he was unsurpassed, to the crowds who dared to delve into their own fates! After years of providing predictions to those seeking spiritual insight, unveiled secrets, and glimpses into the unknown, he suddenly disappeared! Neither his friends nor neighbors knew what happened to him or where he went.

All of his belongings were left behind and perfectly preserved. Among the magical assortment of divination tools, Tarot cards, his crystal ball, a Spirit board, and other mystical implements was a note that read:

"Another will come and assume my place! All that needs to be known is what's on this table; the crystal ball holds the answers."

Much time had passed, and the carnival was never the same until one special day when, true to the prophesy, someone did come, took on the adventure, and assumed the role of the Auset Gypsy!

This is his story, but soon enough it will be your turn . . .

Let the adventure begin!

THE MAJOR ARCANA

THE FOOL
NUMBER 0

Astrological Associations:

Gemini, Aquarius

Traditional Meaning:

Start of new beginnings. A journey. Adventure and call of the unknown. Naive or inexperienced. Daring. A stranger. Humor and humility. A performer or performance. A moment to take a chance. Test of loyalties. Fresh directions. Playing the Fool, fooling another, or being fooled.

Auset Gypsy Meaning:

That first step taken, yet not knowing where Fate could lead. Following a dream and ignoring all of the realities. Going it alone and learning to trust intuition and how to learn from mistakes. Practice makes perfect. How others perceive someone who is different, unique, and true to their personal convictions. Putting it all out there for chance, for humiliation, or victory. Doing without knowing or overthinking, learning consequences after the fact. Boldly and blindly going after one's destiny without a stable plan.

Story Plot:

A stranger appears out of nowhere to a new and very magical place. Surveying the landscape and looking toward unknown horizons. Investigating where the first place to begin his adventure should be. Choosing a direction in seeking out his destiny! Equipped with a sackful of metaphysical implements, a funny-faced little pug named Mr. BoJangles, and pure ambition. From our view of the background, much foreshadowing predicts up-and-coming encounters, places, and characters. His next step begins the adventure and journey . . .

12 — AUSET GYPSY TAROT

THE FOOL

THE MAJOR ARCANA — 13

THE MAGICIAN

NUMBER 1

Astrological Associations:

Mercury, Uranus

Traditional Meaning:

Trickster. Trickery. Jack of all trades, master of none. Ceremony or ritual. Multiple skills. As above, so below. Ceremonial magician. Illusion and disillusionment. Things are not what they seem. A mage. A showman. Self-learning. Metaphysics. Not stationary. Responsibility.

Auset Gypsy Meaning:

A magic man. Charismatic and a charmer. Rogue philosopher. Magical influencer. Magic is afoot. Unconventional thinking. Discovering inner powers. Coming into one's own. Sensitive, intuitive, yet logical and reasonable. Experienced with the occult. Manipulator of unseen forces and metaphysical powers. Foresight, intuition, and determination. Multitasking. Good at many things.

Story Plot:

Our charismatic hero the Auset Gypsy! He's balancing the elements and practicing his skills in magic and intuition. Surrounding him are all the tools necessary for the many adventures that lie ahead. The Cup of Water, the Sword of Air, the Wand of Fire, and the Coins of Earth. Through the use of the crystal ball, Tarot cards, palmistry, and astrology, he displays knowledge of magic, truth, and vision. He becomes the bridge between the physical and spiritual worlds. He proves that knowing how to balance the powers of above and below requires handling more than one thing at a time.

THE MAJOR ARCANA — 15

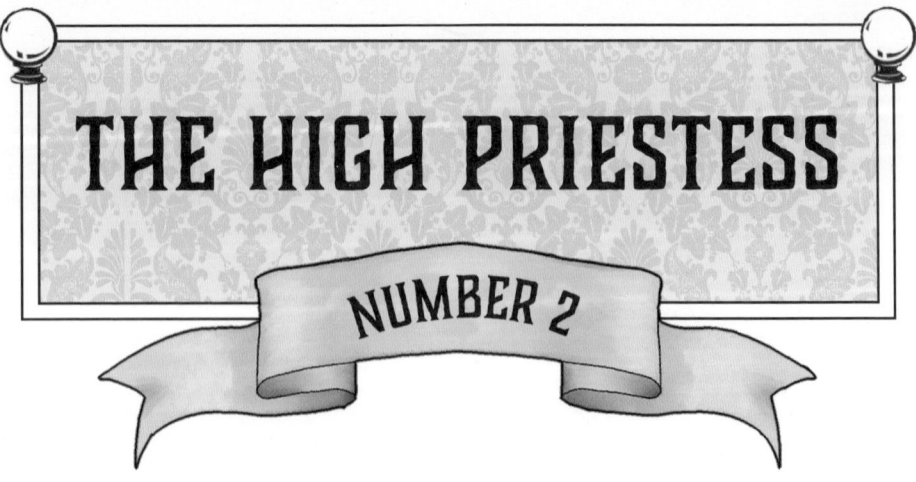

THE HIGH PRIESTESS

NUMBER 2

Astrological Associations:

Moon, Cancer

Traditional Meaning:

Secretive woman. Hidden forces. Clairvoyance. Psychic. Spiritual person. Protected by occult or metaphysical forces. Knowledgeable in divination. Seeking arcane wisdom. Untrusting individual or woman. Controlling from behind the scenes. Hearing a calling.

Auset Gypsy Meaning:

Representative of the Goddess. Woman devoted to spiritual practices and service. Dreams or dream interpretation. Advice or advisor. Intuitive woman. Sacred. Sacred vows. Just out of reach. Nonphysical reality. Gifted psychic. Secrets and confessions. Custodian of the temple of the Goddess. Bestowing important insight.

Story Plot:

Hidden away in a private tent, we find the High Priestess. Dreamy and aloof, looking past what's in front of her, almost in a trance! She is our gentle sibyl named Aradia, a seer and psychic guide. Tending to those who seek her out, she provides counsel to the brave who are willing to listen and heed her words. She is custodian of the library at the Temple of Isis, and only she knows where it is. She talks in riddles and rhymes, so reading between the lines is a must!

THE MAJOR ARCANA — 17

THE EMPRESS

NUMBER 3

Astrological Associations:

Venus, Taurus

Traditional Meaning:

The Goddess. Mother Goddess. Motherhood. Wife. Divine feminine. The earth. Nature. Life giving. Compassion. Love and affection. Healing. Fertility and fertile. Temptation. Pregnancy. Receptive. All giving. Bountiful. Passive. Kindness. Gentile. Queen. Love. Passion.

Auset Gypsy Meaning:

The Goddess Isis. Wisdom. Goddess. Power. A person or child's mother. Love and passion in a relationship. True love. Pure love. Seduction. Romance. Powerful woman. Authoritative woman. Muse and inspiration. Art. Desire. Dream come true. Wife. Lover.

Story Plot:

Isis, Goddess of 10,000 Names, is our Empress. Seen here in her temple with Harpocrates, her son. Benevolent and all loving, she is Mother Nature and Mistress of Fate! With a look on her face of understanding mixed with reluctance and compassion. She knows everyone's destiny. Her power is unparalleled and she bestows wisdom, knowledge, and power upon her devotees. An ever-present spirit assisting adventurers onward toward their goals, with a motion of her hand she can change the course of the stars.

18 —— AUSET GYPSY TAROT

THE EMPRESS

THE MAJOR ARCANA — 19

THE EMPEROR

NUMBER 4

Astrological Associations:

Aries, Jupiter

Traditional Meaning:

Absolute power. Keen judgment. Generosity. Control. Politics. Male authority. Father. Bestowing. Challenge. Winning. Truth be known. Honesty. Family man. The God. Divine masculine. Judge. Employer. Husband. Kindness. Lightning. Temperate. Trust. Financial gain. Success. Warrior. Soldier.

Auset Gypsy Meaning:

Giving and generous. New money. Business and enterprise. Entrepreneur. Success. Good fortune. Streak of luck and popularity. Recognized publicly.
Ambition. Great idea combined with determination pays off. Mix business and pleasure. Rewards.

Story Plot:

High above the carnival on the mountain, we find the Emperor. Looking down on the activities and routines of all the inhabitants below. He is called Jupiter Amun to some and Serapis, or Zeus, to others. He favors our hero's personal tenacity and bestows rewards on those honorable enough to be forthcoming! With his eagle messenger Ganymede at his side and a magical, never-ending fortuitous sack of Coins of Earth in his hand. Fortune favors the bold, and the bold receive accolades and merit for their help.

THE MAJOR ARCANA

THE HIEROPHANT

NUMBER 5

Astrological Associations:

Neptune, Pisces

Traditional Meaning:

Priest. Priestly work. Reverend. Honorable and spiritual man. Organizer. Wise. Teacher. Removed from society. Charitable worker. Holy person. Custodian of the temple. Spiritual practice right. Enforces the law. Well versed in religion. Listens. Words of wisdom. Honors the Gods. Purity.

Auset Gypsy Meaning:

Learned in spiritual practice and tradition. Upholds traditions. Book smart. Well versed in ritual. Teaches the law. Observes the sacred holidays. Tends to animals. Respectable authority on spiritual arts and practices. Performs acts on behalf of the public. Protects arcane knowledge from profane misuse.

Story Plot:

The Hierophant Mithras is in his proper setting and tending to the Temple of Isis. Taking care of the sacred Ibis Thoth and offering sacrifices in ceremonious ritual on behalf of an absent public. Astute and serious in his role as spiritual liaison of the Gods and administer of ancient tradition to the public, his presence is both revered and anticipated. Sharing his knowledge of ritual and communication with spirits and Gods comes only after serious dedicated initiation.

THE MAJOR ARCANA — **23**

THE LOVERS
NUMBER 6

Astrological Associations:

Venus, Mars

Traditional Meaning:

Contracts. Marriages. Union. Sex. Couple. Mergers. Partnerships. Collaborations. Compatibility. Romantics. Romance. Courting. Dating. Uncommitted couple. Two become one. Dowry. Agreements. Arrangements. Happiness. Friendship. Unrequited love.

Auset Gypsy Meaning:

Passion and romance. Love. A happy couple. Unbreakable commitment. Romantic liaison. Physical intimacy. Close friends. Love at first sight. Kindred spirits. Attracted to one another. Opposites attract. Sexual tensions. Flirtation. Love finds a way. Happily ever after.

Story Plot:

On a stage, two performers play out the love affair between Venus, the Goddess of Love, and Mars, the Warrior God. Confusing themselves for the actual Gods themselves, these actors fall madly in love with each other as Cupid aims his arrow to cinch the deal! At this very moment, the Lovers become one and the romance and passion they share becomes real, convincing the audience that true love does in fact conquer all. Especially when we least expect it.

24 —— AUSET GYPSY TAROT

THE LOVERS

THE MAJOR ARCANA — 25

THE CHARIOT

NUMBER 7

Astrological Associations:

Mars, Sagittarius

Traditional Meaning:

Travel. Long journeys. Forward motion. High ambition. Soldier. War. Parades. Mystery float in a passion parade. Movement. Loss of control. Regaining control. Getting someplace quick. Long distance. Automobiles. Accidents. News. Public recognition.

Auset Gypsy Meaning:

Getting ahead faster than anticipated. Receiving attention. Travel. Responsibility. Control over one's actions. Military, police, or EMT forces. Events. A car. Transportation. Balance of duality to work in ones favor. A race. Competition. Test of skills.

Story Plot:

Our Hero needs to cover a lot of ground, and fast! With his counterpart Mr. Bojangles the Pug at his side, they set out to accomplish the mission. Meeting the public, gaining popular recognition, and sharing his metaphysical divination skills en masse. The open roads call; it's time to accept the challenge of the unknown and compete! However, mastering one's direction and trust of intuition requires experience. This wagon is pulled by a white unicorn denoting modesty and moderation, whereas the black Pegasus wants to fly instead of trod, be free, and go buck wild! If not careful, decisions between want and need could get out of control easily.

26 —— AUSET GYPSY TAROT

THE MAJOR ARCANA — 27

JUSTICE

NUMBER 8

Astrological Associations:

Libra, Jupiter

Traditional Meaning:

Obeying metaphysical, natural, and man-made law. To maintain centeredness. Karma. Social justice. Court hearings. Problems with the law. Lawyers. Deliberation. Logic. Providing evidence. The truth comes out no matter what. Testimony.

Auset Gypsy Meaning:

Balancing the mind and heart through reason. The zodiac sign of Libra. Autumn equinox. Time period when all in existence is judged and receives rewards or punishments for deeds done prior. The Goddess Athena. Explore peaceful methods to obtain a solution. Consider both sides of a story before jumping to conclusions. Sound mind, centered heart.

Story Plot:

The Goddess Athena holds the scales of infinity and measures the heart against the feather, an ancient Egyptian belief of how karma works. The heart must remain lighter than the feather! Keep a light heart! She also holds the Sword of Air, which becomes an extension of the will depending on how it is used. Her loyal familiar, the owl Bubo, sees in all directions; all good deeds are seen and no deception is out of sight. The curtains of the Sun and Moon obscure the corridor behind her. These represent the measure of time in days and nights and the importance of balancing how we spend our time.

THE MAJOR ARCANA

THE HERMIT

NUMBER 9

Astrological Associations:

Saturn, Virgo

Traditional Meaning:

Outsider. Beggar. Outcast. A stranger. Elderly person. Saturn. Heretic. Distrusted person. Wise person. Recluse. Eccentric. Believer in superstition or outdated ways of thinking. One who doesn't follow current trends. Ostracized. Mysterious individual. Time. Hidden identity.

Auset Gypsy Meaning:

Privacy. Hidden mystic. Protector of hidden knowledge. Requiring time alone for study or practice. Observer. Differing opinions. A mature teacher. Removed from pop culture. An astrologer. An individual thinker. Alchemist. Experienced master. An everyday person with excellent advice. Advice in the least likely place. The Saturn return.

Story Plot:

The Hermit isn't easily found and must be sought out! Sometimes only by divine intervention will paths cross. He keeps his identity hidden and a secret. He chooses whom and how to advise his known or unbeknown students. Spending most of his time sequestered away in his astrolab tower studying metaphysical science and biology! He knows things most people never will. He doesn't push an agenda of philosophy; instead he shares it when the moment is right, and he teaches through myth or allegory. He appears as quickly as he disappears, coming and going as he pleases. A proficient ceremonial magician and healer is evident by the Was scepter he wields.

AUSET GYPSY TAROT

THE MAJOR ARCANA — 31

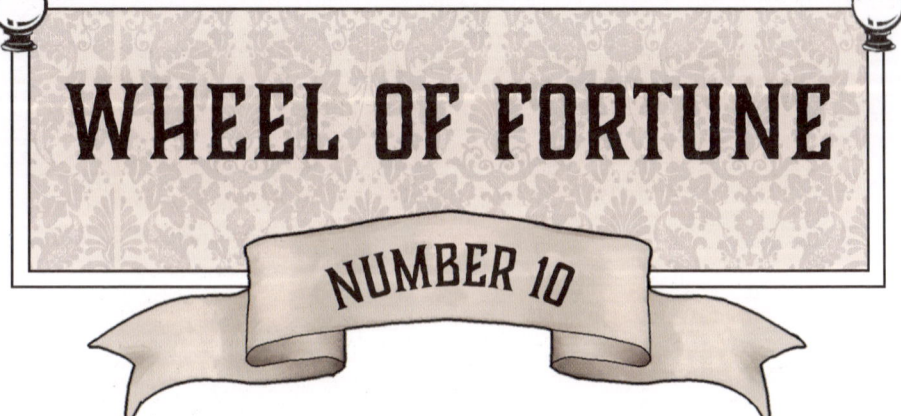

WHEEL OF FORTUNE

NUMBER 10

Astrological Associations:

Jupiter, Venus

Traditional Meaning:

Lady Luck. Good luck and fortune. Taking blind chances. Spinning the wheel of life. Gambling. Indecision and letting fate decide. High odds. Going up against the odds. Hoping for the best. Accepting any inevitable outcome. Outside forces being in control of direction or outcome. Powerlessness. Risk. Seeing where life ends up without decision-making.

Auset Gypsy Meaning:

Excitement and betting against Fate. Taking a chance on winning big without applying effort. Feeling lucky. The Wheel of Life spinning in new directions. Destiny still has yet to be seen. Anxiousness and hope. Waiting for an outcome. Accepting whatever comes your way the best way possible. Influencing Lady Luck. Feeling out of control. Our stars determine the way, no matter how hard we try to change our path.

Story Plot:

Lady Luck or Fortuna appears as a glamorous showgirl roulette handler! Offering various prizes in all of her hands. One is humble humility in the form of a lotus; a golden rudder is another, to steer through the seas of life with ease; another hand lifts her blindfold, thus cheating and seeing who's before her; and her other hand holds the Wheel of Fate as it spins eternally. Until it's your turn to play and take a chance to find out where it lands. Below the wheel are all the coins of Earth that players have lost when waging Fortuna for her blessing, still waiting to be won!

32 —— AUSET GYPSY TAROT

WHEEL OF FORTUNE

THE MAJOR ARCANA — 33

STRENGTH

NUMBER 11

Astrological Associations:

Leo, Virgo

Traditional Meaning:

Courage. Fervor. Wrestling with personal issues. Leo. Mother Nature. Taming the wild beast. Confrontation. Challenge and victory. Facing fears. Taking a forceful approach. Heat of summer. Battle. Struggle. Going up against the odds. Proof of strength.

Auset Gypsy Meaning:

The Dance. To apply force or to show grace. Being put on display. Overcoming almost impossible situations. Test of strength. The labors of Hercules. Balance of play and hard work. Going about a solution in other ways. Confidence and vigor. Fortune favors the bold. Beauty and the beast. Cusp of Leo and Virgo.

Story Plot:

A lion tamer shows an audience that even the mightiest of beasts can be tamed through kindness, patience, and discipline. With a playful smile on her face and a mighty roar from the lion's mouth, these two end their act in a dance between humanity and the animal kingdom. Roses, daisies, and lotus flowers are flung at the performers as a bravo from the audience; this floral symbolism consists of spirituality, love, and innocence. This act or routine is reenacted daily and multiple times a day, showing that trust and determination to overcome impossible odds are possible but take time.

STRENGTH

THE MAJOR ARCANA — 35

THE HANGED MAN

NUMBER 12

Astrological Associations:

Neptune, Aquarius

Traditional Meaning:

Criminal. Punishment. Wrongdoing. Poor decisions. Breaking the law. Outlaw. Suffering. Sacrifice. Paying the price for an offense. Learning the hard way. Material excess. End of life. Tree of life. Incarceration. Wrongful incarceration. Betrayal. False friendship.

Auset Gypsy Meaning:

No good deed goes unpunished! Stuck between decisions. Torment. Frustration. Fear. Another point of view. Mistrust. Contemplation. Stuck between here and there. Letting go of what doesn't serve. Remembering what matters. Powerless. Submission. Meditation. Alternative solutions. Self-sacrifice. Enlightenment via uncomfortable circumstances.

Story Plot:

How did our hero end up here? Poor choices? Was it voluntary? Was he tricked into such a vulnerable and uncomfortable position? Possibly a mix of all the above. He's lost the shirt off his back, not to mention his pants too! His magical accoutrements are just out of reach and with no help in sight. Naked and alone, he'll have to rely on patience, meditation, and self-reliance to get out of this bind. The two views behind him are of the cemetery and the tower high upon a hill, where clouds seem to part, showing that hope is found in the distance. Take heed of the phrase in Latin at the top of the card reads, "The bitter truth is better than the sweetest lies."

THE MAJOR ARCANA — 37

DEATH (DANCE MACABRE)

NUMBER 13

Astrological Associations:

Scorpio, Pluto

Traditional Meaning:

Physical death. New life. Dying. Specters. Ghosts. The end. Life's end. The completion of a cycle. Setting one free of material trappings. The underworld. The great beyond. The grave.

Auset Gypsy Meaning:

Death. To end a life. Restless spirits. Spectral influence. Listening for spirits. Expiration. Expiration dates. Point of no return. Time is over. Warnings. Danger.

Story Plot:

A gloomy cemetery is cheered up some when Death the Grim Reaper comes through playing a violin. Eerie romantic notes float in the air, where he is followed by entranced ballerinas. This grim ensemble performs the Dance Macabre in hopes of attracting more followers in joining them, in one way or another. Death, this nefarious character, is just doing what's in his nature. Neither good or evil, Death executes his job perfectly and meticulously on time! Beware of hearing his deadly melody.

THE MAJOR ARCANA

TEMPERANCE

NUMBER 14

Astrological Associations:

Aquarius, Pisces

Traditional Meaning:

Moderation. Balance. Calm. Centering. Mind and soul. Body and spirit. Sun and Moon. Day and night. Male and female. Receptive and assertive. Human and animal. Perfection. Maintaining polarity. Good and bad.

Auset Gypsy Meaning:

Holding both heart and mind. Being of two planes at one time. Living a double existence. Bringing peace and calm to turbulent situations. Maintaining the spiritual life and mundane physical life. Applying moderation in all things. Mediation and bliss.

Story Plot:

The Mermaid sits on the border of light and dark. Holding the Cups of Water and both receiving and returning the flows of the waters of life back into the cycles for eternity. Her place is of extreme importance; being part human and part of the natural world, she possesses the even keel needed to maintain the flooding waters of all existence in a continual flow. Keeping not a drop for herself, she channels the flow of spirit, matter, thought, emotion, and intuition perpetually.

40 — **AUSET GYPSY TAROT**

THE MAJOR ARCANA — 41

THE DEVIL

NUMBER 15

Astrological Associations:

Saturn, Capricorn

Traditional Meaning:

Evil. Villain. Wicked. Negative. Violent. Ungodly. Impure. Immoral. Bad manners. Out of control. Greediness. Gluttony. Selfishness. Addiction. Possession. Hateful. Lord of darkness. Corruptible. Hell. Soulless. Demonic. Lies. Wrongdoing. Intentional hurt.

Auset Gypsy Meaning:

Trouble. Temptation. Giving into one's dark side. Living too close to the edge. Unredeemable. When greed takes over. Being consumed with selfishness. Causing pain without any remorse. Powers of evil looking for outlets. Excess in behavior. Want at any cost.

Story Plot:

The Devil assumes pleasing appearances, as learned here. Seductive, alluring, and all-around wicked. These two characters are really one entity that uses whatever tricks necessary to undermine the pure of heart. Ever present to deter the adventurer from seeking their rightful destiny, this dark presence tempts the best of them with fleeting fame and misfortune at a very high price! Amid the checkered floor of false initiation is the distorted broken mirror of mistruth, and two green false flames of disinformation and corrupt knowledge. Enter if you dare!

THE DEVIL

THE MAJOR ARCANA — 43

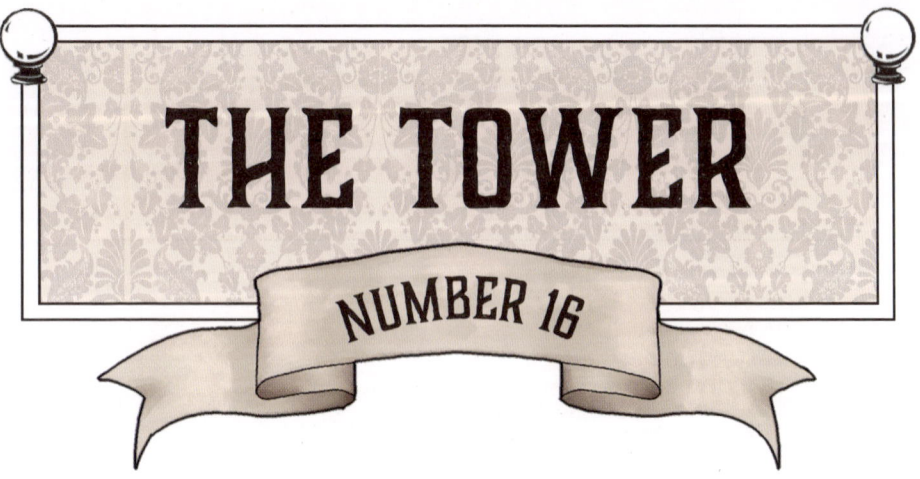

THE TOWER

NUMBER 16

Astrological Associations:

Pluto, Neptune

Traditional Meaning:

Destruction. Repentance. Sudden disruption. Security fail. Losing everything. Freedom. The material world submitting to the natural and spiritual powers. Out of control. Falling from grace. Loss of illusionary material possessions. Being exposed. Unsafe.

Auset Gypsy Meaning:

Reaching heights. Immovable challenges. Sanctuary. Prison. Astrolab. Beacon of hope. Better vantage point. Forces of fate. Stronghold. Mystery. Beckoning.

Story Plot:

The parting of clouds around The Tower gives hope that there is a calm in the storm. Lightning from the heavens striking the iron canopy atop the tower is either destroying it with fire or fueling it with fire and electricity. This is the mystery! The energies swirling around this structure consist of powerful elements. An astrology clock on its facade denotes this may be an astrolab for mapping and consulting the zodiac. A shadowy figure of a person can be seen on a very high ledge monitoring the massive storm or calling on these elements ceremoniously via ritual to the Tower itself.

44 —— AUSET GYPSY TAROT

THE MAJOR ARCANA — 45

THE STAR

NUMBER 17

Astrological Associations:

Aquarius, Leo

Traditional Meaning:

Faith. Hope. Summer. Wishful thinking. Wishes. Messages. Light at the end of the tunnel. Darkest before dawn. Magic. Distance. Astrology. Precision. Eternal. Travel. Night skies. Astral powers. Navigation. Wonder. Time.

Auset Gypsy Meaning:

Rising of Sothis. The Dog Star. Zodiac sign of Aquarius. True friendship and trust. Wishes come true. Dreams are still on the horizon. Secret messages. Travel to faraway places. Inspiration and creativity. Spiritual connection and magic of the spheres. Summer solstice.

Story Plot:

The Witches of Goddess Hecate perform an ancient rite related to the raising of the star Sothis. Taking on the spiritual affinities of the Goddess, they serve to pour forth the rising waters overflowing into all the levels of existence. These waters of spiritual knowledge, mystical philosophy, magic, and inspiration. Apart from the Cups, these Witches hold the ritual keys and torches sacred to Hecate to traverse both the natural word and the underworld in their rite. It is truly darkest before dawn, a time to put trust in what can't be seen and even a little magic.

THE MAJOR ARCANA —— 47

THE MOON

NUMBER 18

Astrological Associations:

Cancer, Moon

Traditional Meaning:

Sorcery. Magic. Dreams. Dream interpretation. Light in darkness. Illusions. Cast spells. Desire. Lunacy. Instinct. Time for magic. Deception. Witchcraft. Unseen powers. Making wishes. Romance but not true love. Divine feminine influences. Free woman.

Auset Gypsy Meaning:

Being led by feel and intuition. Following messages in dreams. Warns against danger. Being allowed to see only what's in front of you. Goddess Diana or Artemis. Nature at night. Not to fear what can't been seen. Higher intuition. Psychic visions and dreams.

Story Plot:

The Moon in all her glory is accompanied by Diana, Goddess of the moon and wild hunt. Her loyal hound at her side to assist in the pursuit of whatever it is she is chasing. In the distance are the Moon Towers, a portal and magical place where one can walk toward the stars. Beyond these towers to the west waits the Underworld. Jasmine flowers appear, sharing their intoxicating scent to add a romantic scent and create a dreamlike state under a starry night. It's a truly magical moment when dreams and ideas are born and fantasies come to life. We can see only what light the phase of the moon offers, and that's all we need to see at this moment.

48 —— AUSET GYPSY TAROT

THE MOON

THE MAJOR ARCANA — 49

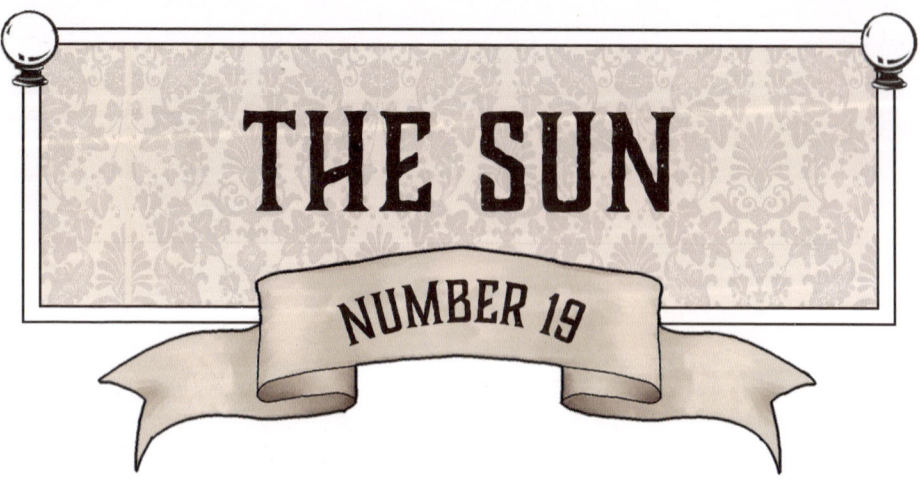

THE SUN

NUMBER 19

Astrological Associations:

Sun, Leo

Traditional Meaning:

Popularity. Good health. Attention. Ego. Excelling. Grace. Accolades. Public recognition.
Strong talent. Athletics, academia, and music. Champion. Highest awards received.
New life. Poetry. Writing. Articulate. Attractiveness. Outstanding. Arrogant. Outshines.

Auset Gypsy Meaning:

Happiest moment in life. Achieving recognition for accomplishing personal goals.
Vitality and high energy. Physically fit and healthy. Strong body. Sharing.
Inspirational. Someone who shines for their spirit and personality. Perfect light.
Truth. Nothing hidden.

Story Plot:

Apollo, frequently recognized as the Sun, offers hymns and prose to the actual sun
above him in the sky. Surrounded by sunflowers, we seem to be in the height of
summer, feelings are high, and it's a perfect moment. Friend of the Muses, Apollo
holds a lyre reminding us that vibration and sound create, heal, and are the music
of the spheres. Full of life and vitality, he offers inspiration, abundance of energy, and
a warmth to the soul. The darkest times have passed; we can see clearly without
hindrance in all directions with confidence and ease.

THE SUN

THE MAJOR ARCANA — 51

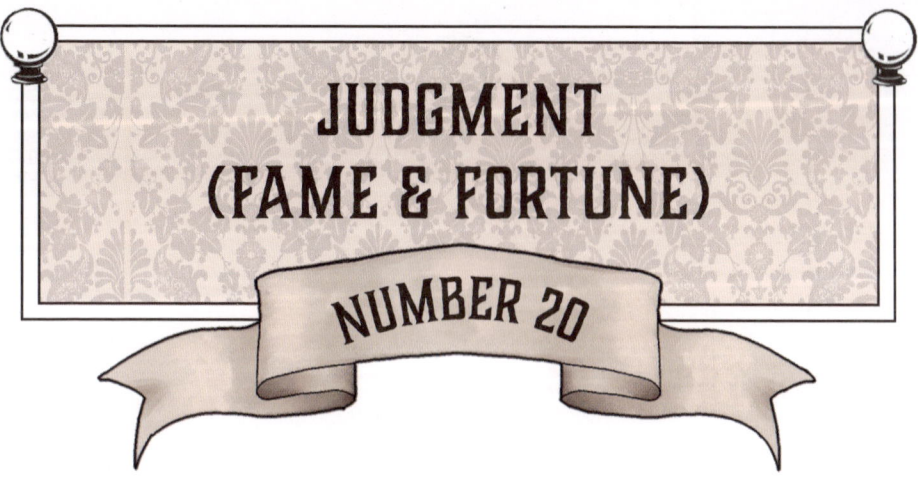

JUDGMENT (FAME & FORTUNE)

NUMBER 20

Astrological Associations:

Mercury, Jupiter

Traditional Meaning:

Fame and fortune. Being called to one's destiny. Hearing the inner voice of truth. Choosing correctly. Intervention. Making wise decisions based on experience or evidence. Higher spiritual awakening. Ones genius brims with great ideas. Waking from the dead. New life. Higher consciousness or divine self is illuminated and recognized.

Auset Gypsy Meaning:

Time to step into our rightful place. Destiny calls. Perfect and divine timing. Spiritual rescue. Eureka moment. The third eye opens. Knowing the truth without influence. Rising to the occasion. Doing the right thing. Following spirit over material falsities. Being called out. Actions taken decide next steps according to Fate; reward or punishment.

Story Plot:

Mercury flies through the sky, blowing his trumpet and holding the Wand of Fire to awaken those chosen to answer the call to their destiny. A powerful moment where what we decide to do next relies on how this heed is answered. A performer comes out of a tent, a woman leaves a cave, and a dead person ascends from a grave in the ground to arrive at their higher calling! Though everyone gets a turn, we don't know when and should be prepared anyway. Mercury announces whose turns it is. Awakening spiritual energies, brilliant new ideas, and coming into recognition publicly.

52 — AUSET GYPSY TAROT

JUDGMENT

THE MAJOR ARCANA — 53

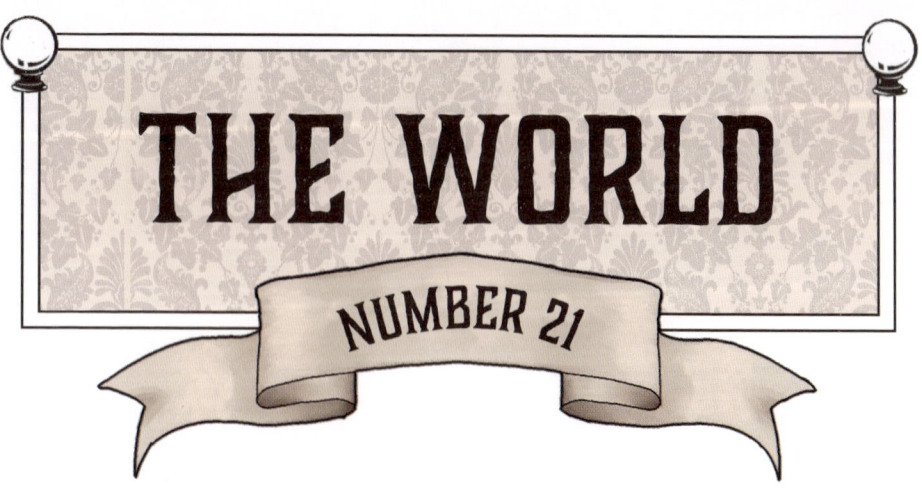

THE WORLD

NUMBER 21

Astrological Associations:

Leo, Aquarius, Jupiter, Scorpio

Traditional Meaning:

Attainment of the Mysteries. Initiation, reaching finalization. Goals accomplished. Rebirth. Transcendence. Public recognition. Mastering skills. Graduation. Travel. Making it to the end of a journey. Success. Accomplishment. Spiritual attainment. Rewards.

Auset Gypsy Meaning:

Achievement in long-term challenges and goals. Purification. Arriving on the scene. Receiving due accolades for a job well done. Obtaining esoteric knowledge and using it wisely. End of a chapter. The step before starting all over. Divine and public acknowledgment.

Story Plot:

Our Hero completes his mission! Surviving trials and tribulations, then overcoming stacked odds both spiritually and physically. He arrives to public recognition. Emerging from his tent, he's greeted by the Gods and crowds exhibiting the signs of attainment received for such an arduous but worthwhile journey, like those before him and those yet to come. Carrying the lotus wand of spiritual awareness and the double-wicked candle of esoteric and exoteric wisdom, wearing the pure white sash of Isis, revealing his initiation into the divine mysteries and surrounded by the laurel wreaths of victory and success! He's proven himself worthy to play the role between the spiritual and material worlds and utilize the metaphysical knowledge and divination skills to the public on their behalf. So our story ends, or does it just begin?
The adventure lives on . . .

THE MAJOR ARCANA

THE MINOR ARCANA

ACE OF CUPS:
Element: Water.
True love. Absolute happiness. Complete abundance. Trust feelings.

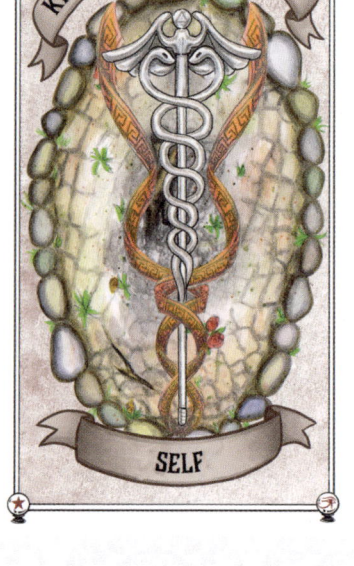

ACE OF WANDS:
Element: Fire
Important message. Life-changing news. Take action.

THE MINOR ARCANA

ACE OF COINS:
Element: Earth

Success and achievement. Highest material rewards. Money.

ACE OF SWORDS:
Element: Air
Willpower. Acceptance of a challenge. Diplomacy and clear judgment.

58 — AUSET GYPSY TAROT

2 OF CUPS:
Venus in Cancer
Not exactly love at first sight, but love that develops. Loyalty. New relationship. Allies. Kindred spirits. Intuition and feelings. Companions.

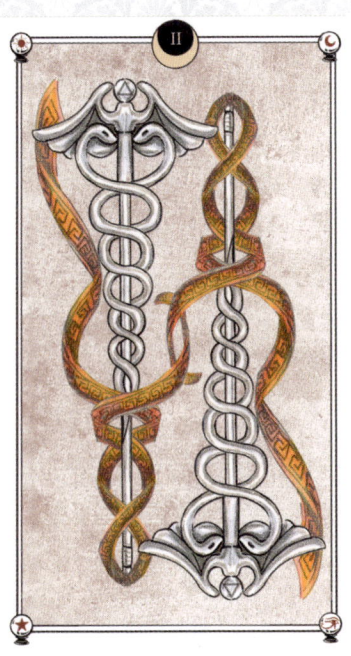

2 OF WANDS:
Mars in Aries
Horizons of the past and future. Being present. Choices made now influence near future. Choices that require immediate action. Somewhere between here and there. Opportunities in the distance.

2 OF COINS:
Jupiter in Capricorn

Excellent business partnership. Doing two things at once. Money split evenly. Strong work ethic. A price is doubled. Business mergers.

2 OF SWORDS:
Moon in Libra

Personal initiation. Scissors. Cut away that which does not serve. Severing of partnership. Division. Split in ideas. Going up against an equal adversary. Strategy. Defend or protect.

3 OF CUPS:
Mercury in Cancer

Happiness and good times. Love overcoming the odds. A love triangle. Autumn season. Family and friends coming together to celebrate. Wedding or birth. Overabundance of emotions.

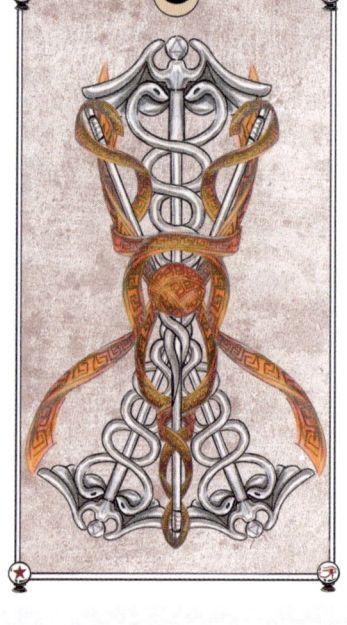

3 OF WANDS:
Sun in Aries

Blocks in the road to success. Obstacles. Need help of others. Strength in numbers. Unexpected surprises. Necessary steps toward achieving a goal. Getting in one's own way.

3 OF COINS:
Mars in Capricorn

Recognition for talents. Multiple job offers. Being invited to be part of a team. A silent partner is needed. Triple the risk, triple success possible. Solid business advice. Growing prosperity.

3 OF SWORDS:
Saturn in Libra

Ultimate disappointment. Brokenheartedness. Strife. Bitter argument. Unfortunate news. Sad moment. Deep wound. Clash of ideas has no positive outcome.

4 OF CUPS:
Moon in Cancer

Boredom. Uninspired. Tantrum. Harboring ill intent or disarming feelings. Secrets. Emotional burden. Disinterested. Emotionally cut off. Trust bad feeling. Time alone to feel things out.

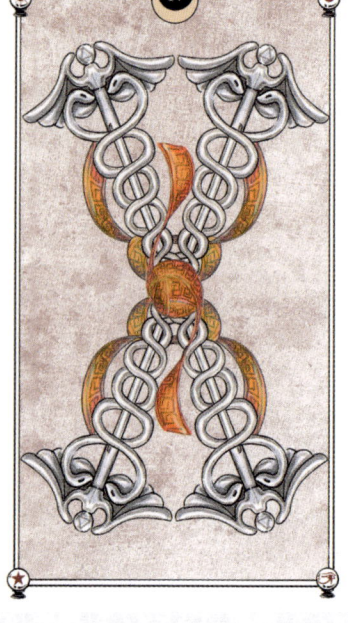

4 OF WANDS:
Venus in Aries

Happy home. House in which one lives. Holidays or traditions carried out in the home. Physical repair or construction to the home. New home. Physically strong. Good health. Newlyweds.

THE MINOR ARCANA

4 OF COINS:
Sun in Capricorn

Solid foundation physically, materially, and spiritually. Concrete evidence. Financially stable. Flowing income. Honest but unpleasant advice, practicality over eccentricity. Expenses covered.

4 OF SWORDS:
Jupiter in Libra

Sleep. Rest required. Calm the mind of overactive thoughts. Meditation. Answers found in dreams. Silence. Time to one's self. Allow moment of contemplation. Clear thoughts required.

5 OF CUPS:
Mars in Scorpio

Regrettable decisions. Resentment over the past. Distrust in love. Hateful feelings. Lies. Separation. Unhappiness. Depression. Spiritual distress. Abandonment. Anger. Lust.

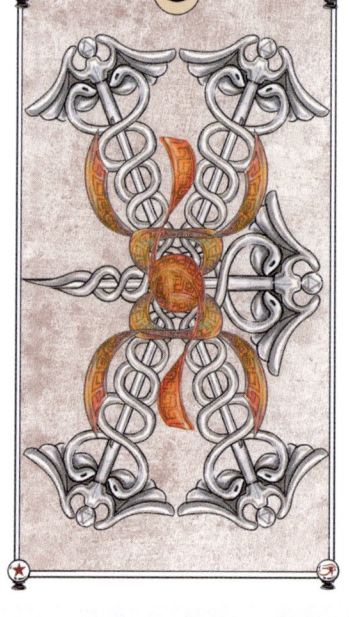

5 OF WANDS:
Saturn in Leo

Disagreements between teammates. Competition and proving worth. Infighting. Force and action required over diplomacy and passiveness. Big competition. Too many cooks in the kitchen. Poor leadership.

5 OF COINS:
Mercury in Taurus

Financial misfortune. Bad luck. Fast loss of income. Lost job. Stress. Illness. Imbalance spiritually resulting physically. Money pit. Gambling and losing. Stolen property. Money lent isn't returned.

5 OF SWORDS:
Venus in Aquarius

Playing mediator. Differences of opinion cause strife. Trying to reconcile after an argument. Distance occurs between others over disagreement. Not a time to apply magic or perform metaphysical operations.

6 OF CUPS:
Sun in Scorpio

The past comes back to remind you, feelings of going back in time. Reuniting with old friends. Rekindling an old flame with a former love. Repeating history. Similar situations. Karma. Second chances. Opportunity to do something over.

6 OF WANDS:
Jupiter in Leo

Victory. Personal success. Advanced public recognition. New job. Receiving a notable title. Beating the odds. Celebrating someone else's triumph. Sincere motives. Fifteen minutes of fame.

THE MINOR ARCANA —— 67

6 OF COINS:
Moon in Taurus

A bit of unexpected good luck. Giving back and charity. Patience and grace pays off. Prosperity and accolades distributed evenly. Autumn equinox. Karma.

6 OF SWORDS:
Mercury in Aquarius

Cleaning up a mess. Getting away with it. Happily walking away. Tidying up loose ends before moving on. Collecting what's needed to know in order to advance. Accepting responsibilities.

7 OF CUPS:
Venus in Scorpio

Almost perfect. Content. Too many choices. Feelings of being overwhelmed. Personal moment to prioritize dreams, career, family, love, or home. Choose wisely. Lucky moment. Uncanny meeting.

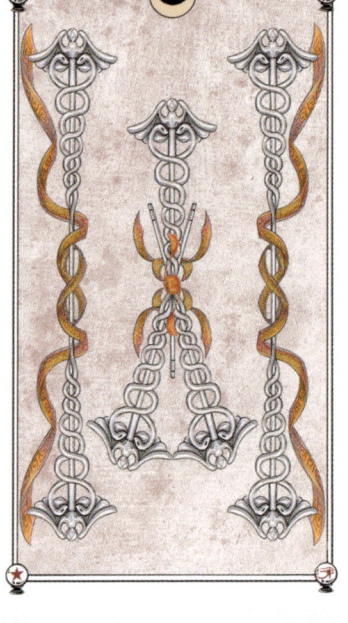

7 OF WANDS:
Mars in Leo

Defend your spot. Be physically prepared to stand your ground. Take on the odds. Many things coming at once. Feeling surrounded. Trust. If something needs to be done right, do it yourself.

THE MINOR ARCANA

7 OF COINS:
Saturn in Taurus

Make sure to save a little something for yourself. Dedication and hard work pays off. Seeing the outcome of pure diligence. Creating something from nothing. Multiple business opportunities. Feelings of self-satisfaction.

7 OF SWORDS:
Moon in Aquarius

Travel. Escape. Fantasy. Follow a good idea no matter where it leads. Leaving old concepts or routines behind. Discovering something new. Don't fear what's unknown. Missing the boat. One door closes and a window opens.

8 OF CUPS:
Saturn in Pisces

Balanced feelings. Perfect love and perfect trust. Romance. Sharing. Fulfillment. Engagements. Senses are heightened. A good time for love spells. Attractiveness. Flirtation. Desire and passion.

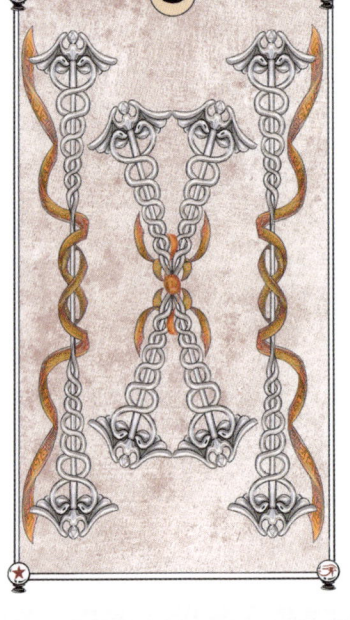

8 OF WANDS:
Mercury in Sagittarius

Clear skies. Easy moments. No hurdles. Actions go smoothly without any restrictions. Playful times. Fun. No unexpected circumstances. Target reached. Anything applied is effortless. Synchronization. Focus on breath. Exercise.

THE MINOR ARCANA

8 OF COINS:
Sun in Virgo

Consistent and comfortable amount of work. Being able to tackle projects and workloads with ease. Skills put to good use. Doing what is loved. Maintaining a positive stream of good luck mixed with making dreams reality. Making things by hand becomes profitable.

8 OF SWORDS:
Jupiter in Gemini

Keeping calm in dangerous or frustrating situations. Centering. Obeying instinct when the way can't be seen. Stuck between the tigers. Maintaining peace through diplomacy. Divine intelligence.

9 OF CUPS:
Jupiter in Pisces
Wishes come true. Magic happens without trying. Charmed life. Being in the spotlight. Be careful of what is wished for because it comes true. A birthday. Destiny. Very strongly placed stars in personal astrology chart. Lucky person.

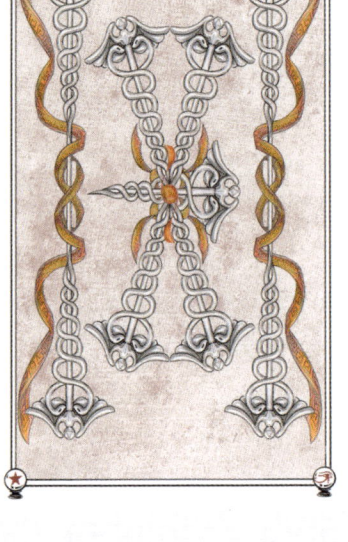

9 OF WANDS:
Moon in Sagittarius
Near endgame. Physical exertion. Running out of energy, standing alone. Headaches. Beware of physical injuries. Time needed to heal and rest. Sitting on the sidelines of life for a moment. Protect yourself magically.

THE MINOR ARCANA

9 OF COINS:
Venus in Virgo

Inheritance. Obtaining successful business or property. Retirement. Enjoying life's efforts and hard work. Winter solstice. Receiving expensive gifts. Finery. Success with art or music. Performer's big break. Nine years from now. The mountains.

9 OF SWORDS:
Mars in Gemini

Mental stress. Nightmare. Loss of sleep. Consumed by uncontrollable thoughts. Haunted by past failures. Forced poor choices. Bad mistakes. Being frustrated. Not wanting to do something. Forgetting something important. Regrettable words exchanged. Severe headaches. Projected bad mojo.

10 OF CUPS:
Mars in Pisces

Happily ever after. Dreams come true. Enjoyment of love, family, and friends. Complete emotional fulfillment. Marriage. Happiest moment to be had.

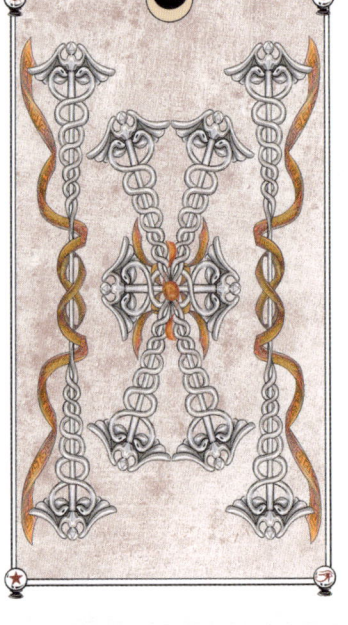

10 OF WANDS:
Saturn in Sagittarius

Overburdened. Overworked. Taking on too many responsibilities of others. Breaking point physically. Pushing the body to the utmost marker. No end in sight. Working too much overtime. Imbalance between physical and spiritual life. Labors of Hercules.

THE MINOR ARCANA

10 OF COINS:
Mercury in Virgo

Property. Buying a house. Selling a house or business for a very large profit. Real estate.
Becoming financially stable later in life. Working from home. In charge of a copious amount of money.

10 OF SWORDS:
Sun in Gemini

Defeat. Outnumbered. Betrayed. Suffering. Sacrifice. Prometheus. One's own thoughts worked against them. Tricked by trustworthy associates. Going too far. Warnings. Beware of traps. Sabotage.

KING OF CUPS
Moon in Cancer

A compassionate man. Father. Quiet and kind. Strong temper when provoked. Older man.

Summer solstice. Remember to think of others' feelings. Sympathetic ear. Seen, not heard.

QUEEN OF CUPS
Pluto in Scorpio

A controlling woman. Trust is earned. Intimidating and demands respect. Gives no second chances. Sensitive feelings and protects them with a biting tongue. A mistress. Has powers.

THE MINOR ARCANA

CAVALIER OF CUPS
Neptune in Pisces

A romantic. Dreamer. Performer. Musician and poet. Gentle and generous. If betrayed, can be spiteful and vengeful. Deep sleeper but still a go-getter. Needs private time. Brings life to a party.

PRINCE/ESS OF CUPS
Element: Water

Preteen or child with polite demeanor. Curious and always listening. Unlimited imagination. Sensitive types with highly attuned intuition. Great second sight and drawn to art, music, and spirituality.

KING OF WANDS
Mars in Aries

Rugged, handsome, and a heartbreaker. Risk taker. Big talker. Doesn't finish what he starts. Witty and intelligent. Likes attention and having followers finish what he can't. Insecure and a big little boy.

QUEEN OF WANDS
Sun in Leo

Stylish and fashionable. Independent woman who can provide for herself. Truth and honesty come first. Work is play, and isn't afraid of hard work. Prefers company of men over women. Falls in love with whom she should not have.

THE MINOR ARCANA

CAVALIER OF WANDS
Jupiter in Sagittarius

The competitor. Takes challenges on for fun. Enjoys popularity. Acts spoiled, and tantrums are expected. Big ego. A soldier or police officer. Learns from mistakes. Great sense of humor. Sexy.

PRINCE/ESS OF WANDS
Element: Fire

Preteen or child with competing nature. Discipline with a mix of love is important. Athletes, sportsmanship, and camaraderie are encouraged. Natural leaders. Do what they want despite warnings.

80 —— AUSET GYPSY TAROT

KING OF COINS
Saturn in Capricorn

Well-respected business man. No nonsense, extremely high work ethic. Takes the long way. Learns the hard way. Love life can be biggest challenge. Self-critical. Generous until taken advantage of. Midlife success. Fiercely stubborn.

QUEEN OF COINS
Venus in Taurus

Excellent business woman. Perfect mother. Faithful wife. Family and values are of utmost importance. She is the power behind the scenes. Conservative but open minded. Earthy person. Practical and nurturing. Mind is almost unchangeable.

CAVALIER OF COINS
Mercury in Virgo

Astute. Determined and detail oriented. Frugal and critical. Reliable and materialistic. Career oriented. Finds pleasure in a bargain. Routine and regiment rule. In love he is committed. Cannot be swayed from convictions.

PRINCE/ESS OF COINS
Element: Earth

Preteen or child who displays early eagerness toward approval and success from a young age. Someone who is willing to put hard work into what they do. Stubborn and impossible to sway.

KING OF SWORDS
Venus in Libra

A lover and romantic. The perfect mix of business and pleasure. A jealous lover if provoked. Brings balance to most situations. Has a humorous personality but can be a worrier. His success comes from ideas and not hard work.

QUEEN OF SWORDS
Uranus in Aquarius

Charismatic and detached. She is a likable type with strong opinions and equally as pertinent willpower. Friendships are golden, and usually her success comes through having friends in the right places. Spiritual but logical, with incredible foresight. Often misunderstood.

THE MINOR ARCANA

CAVALIER OF SWORDS
Mercury in Gemini

Chatty, highly energized, attractive, and quick. He is the first on the scene. Gossip and news reach his ears first. Being quick witted, funny, and somehow endearingly vulnerable are parts of his charm. Enjoys travel and being in the company of interesting people. Young success. Technology.

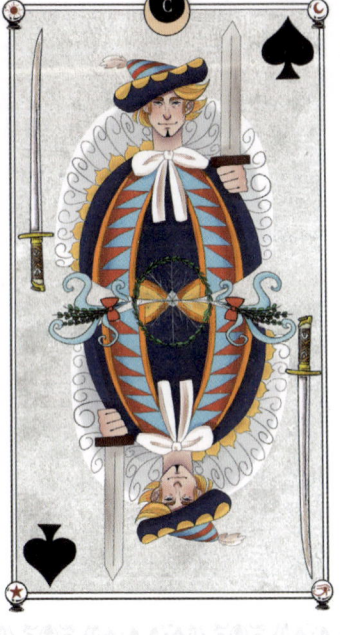

PRINCE/ESS OF SWORDS
Element: Air

Preteen or child seemingly more advanced mentally and spiritually than their peers. Displaying abilities of debate, natural intelligence, and quick frustration when things don't go their way. Mediators and peacekeepers. Truth seekers.

AUSET GYPSY TAROT SPREADS

THE AUSET GYPSY ARADIA LUNAR SPREAD

This spread is used in respect to the Moon and her many phases. Begin the reading with respect to the Moon and the phase she is currently in at the moment. For instance, if the Moon is waning, begin in position 3, what to give up. Continue from there, laying down the next card: position 4 New Moon, hidden factors, etc. This gives an idea of priority and where to grab the spoke of the wheel in the question asked.

1st Position—Waxing Moon: What is coming.

2nd Position—Full Moon: Realization of the question asked, what to do with what has come.

3rd Position—Waning Moon: What needs to be removed or given up to make room for what's come or coming.

4th Position—New Moon: Unseen or hidden factors influencing from behind the scenes. The secret.

5th Position—Flame of Wisdom: The secret lesson learned or reason for the entire journey.

#5

Flame of Wisdom

#1

Waxing Moon

#2

Full Moon

#3

Waning Moon

#4

New Moon

AUSET GYPSY TAROT SPREADS —— 87

AUSET GYPSY SEVEN-POINT-STAR SPREAD

Seven is a very lucky and auspicious number. The Star is a magical symbol. This seven-pointed star is a strong spread for viewing all corners of a situation at one glance.

Position 1—This card reflects what's in the heart of the questioner and influences all the other cards surrounding it. It's the most powerful card.

Position 2—Life at present and around the questioner at the moment. The foundation of the reading.

Position 3—Love, people, places, and things close to the questioner's heart. Emotions and feelings.

Position 4—Health, career, money, the home, good fortune, or physical well-being. All the physical things one can touch.

Position 5—Spiritual corner of life, one's purpose. What inspires one's Muse and the psychic connection.

Position 6—Challenges and hidden troubles. What blocks the questioner or needs to be overcome. Also hidden strengths that are yet to be discovered or solutions to problems found.

Position 7—The future based on the decisions and actions made at the present. What could be! An outcome based on the other cards before it. The crown of the reading.

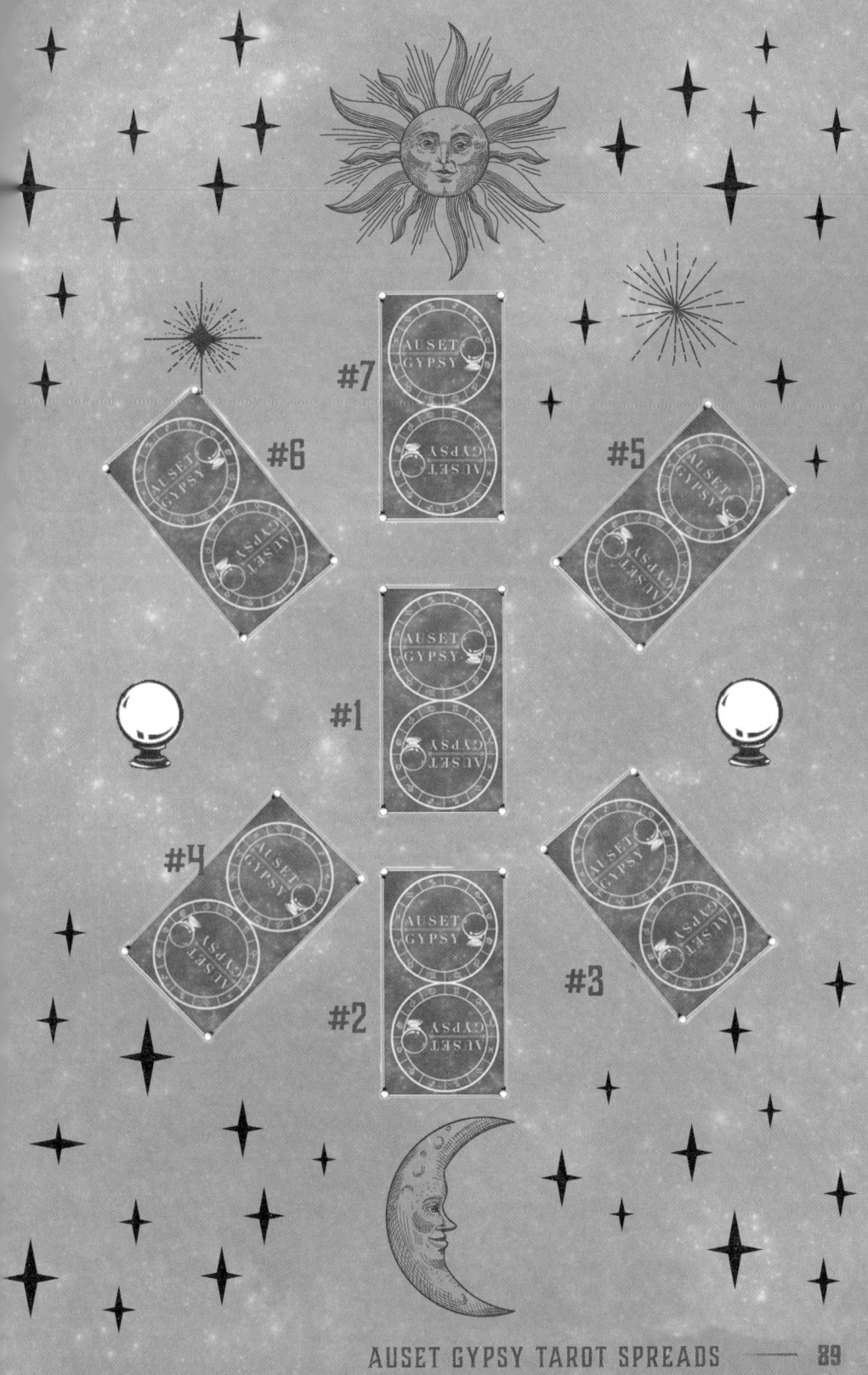

AUSET GYPSY TAROT SPREADS — 89

AUSET GYPSY 3 FATES CARD SPREAD

Sometimes inquiries need direct and to the point answers from the Tarot. Try this simple yet tried and true, effective spread that asks the 3 Fates to answer a question quickly!

Separate the Major Arcana from the Minor Arcana. Shuffle the Major Arcana 3 times and create 3 piles that represent the Past, Present, and Future. Flip the top card over for each of the 3 piles and the Major Arcana card that is revealed influences or dominates the situation spiritually.

Past	Present	Future

Now, shuffle the Minor Arcana 3 times and create 3 piles under each Major Arcana pile. Pull the very last bottom card from the Minor Arcana pile and place on top of the piles. Those Minor Arcana cards will explain the influence of the people, places, and things related to the topic. These 3 cards relate to:

MAJOR ARCANA

MINOR ARCANA

Love   Career   Spiritual

AUSET GYPSY TAROT SPREADS —— 91

AUSET GYPSY TAROT ADVICE, MANTRAS, AND PRACTICES TO LIVE BY AND MEDITATE ON

Here are some words to live by. Apply them when approaching a Tarot reading or when meditating with or without the cards. These words help perpetuate a healthy and balanced spiritual/psychic practice. Say them out loud or to yourself repeatedly like mantras or when preparing to focus for Tarot readings. They create unseen bridges necessary when communicating with the Tarot and they awake the Third Eye. Remember that practice makes perfect!

(Say this when shuffling the deck, out loud or to yourself.)
"May my tongue be silver and my words be golden."

(Ask the Tarot deck and the questioner this before you begin, to break the ice.)
"What good story did you bring to the table?"

(Say and use this when shuffling the Tarot for yourself or someone else.)
"Shuffle once for Love, once for Luck, and once for the Future . . ."

(Perform this meditation regiment to balance the mind and heart and center the self before beginning a Tarot reading.)
Close the eyes. Clear the mind. Breathe in.
Bring attention to the Crown Chakra, Breathe out.
Breathe in, clear the mind a little bit more. Bring attention to the 3rd Eye. Breathe out.
Breathe in one last time. Clear the mind completely. Bring attention to the Heart Chakra. Breathe out.

(Keep in mind these spiritual energies and their properties when handling or shuffling the Tarot deck.)
"Left hand is the Moon, Right hand is the Sun. Moon and Sun, Two Become One."

"Always choose Tarot cards from the deck with the left hand. The left hand is closest to the Heart."

"The Major Arcana are the Fates and Destinies throughout life. The Minor Arcana are the People, Places, and Things."

"Intuition always trumps traditional definitions."

" Love. Thanks. Devotion. All actions should be supported by all three."

"The Tarot is a sacred, choose-your-own-adventure book. Treat it with respect."

NOTES

NOTES

ABOUT THE AUTHOR

Auset Gypsy was the nickname given to James Jacob Pierri when he was a young and charismatic reader at Mystic of the Seven Veils Psychic Venue at Universal Studios while studying at the Florida College of Natural Health & Holistic Sciences. Auset Gypsy transformed from a nickname to a brand, delivering top-quality services to private clientele including celebrities, politicians, authors, athletes, and others. James has had success with his online service; he has appeared on television shows such as MTV's *House of Prophesy*, Bravo's *Housewives of New Jersey*, Psychic Fridays on the WPIX (New York) Morning Show, and theme-related documentaries. Through years of dedication, practice, and the study of metaphysical and occult arts, James has put these skills to good use for clients and in traveling presentations. He gives lectures and talks on a variety of magickal subjects, including candle magic, divination, astrology, Isis mysteries, Wicca, goddess worship, spell casting, and more.